Scattered Blessing

Genesis 11–12 an[illegible] ent Perspecti[illegible]

Richard S Briggs

Principal, Lindisfarne College of Theology

GROVE BOOKS LIMITED

RIDLEY HALL RD CAMBRIDGE CB3 9HU

Contents

Church Mission Society supports the Grove Mission and Evangelism Series
At Church Mission Society, we believe that every Christian is called to join in God's mission, whether that means crossing the street or crossing continents, and we want to set people free to put that call into action.

Dedication
To Richard Harvey

Acknowledgments
I have been thinking about this topic ever since spending four years teaching New Testament, over 20 years ago, in the joyfully multicultural context of All Nations Christian College. It is a delight to dedicate this booklet to my then colleague and long-term friend Richard Harvey, and to thank too the various students there who sharpened up my thinking, including—but not limited to—Amanda Christie, Hazel Frost, Dave and Preeti How and Kuki Rokhum. I am also grateful to 'The Thinklings,' the reading group mentioned in note 31, and especially its host Walter Moberly, for lively discussion of a draft version. Errors and outrageous oversimplifications that remain are mine alone.

First Impression August 2025
ISSN 2399-6536
ISBN 978 1 78827 492 0

Introduction—The Old Testament and Mission

1

This is a short book on a big topic: the Old Testament and mission. I might have liked to call it 'The Old Testament's Vision of Mission,' to match the corresponding Grove booklet by Ian Paul, *The New Testament's Vision of Mission*, but this is a much more modest project, offering a couple of perspectives as a way in to a vast topic.[1]

Instead of trying to be comprehensive I offer two variations on a key theme: that of *blessing*. Much has been said about Gen 12.1–3 and the importance of blessing. I want to argue for a slightly different way of looking at its blessings, partly by placing alongside that passage the immediately preceding one in Gen 11.1–9 about the tower of Babel. The result is an emphasis on what I call 'scattered blessing.'

'Scattered blessing' sounds less proactive and programmatic than the kinds of understandings often taken from Gen 12.1–3, and I see that as a helpful refocusing. But in the end both passages (and many more) are necessary for our vision of the Old Testament and mission. I write in the hope that people involved on the ground in mission work, in and for the church, will find some encouragement and envisioning from the Old Testament. Also, in a personal afterword at the end, I relate what scattered blessing might look like to some of my own ministerial experiences in practice.

Defining Mission in Old Testament Terms

I have resisted the temptation to write at length on matters of definition. Instead here is a brief reflection, with pointers to further reading. Practitioners less interested in defining terms may skip to the next chapter.

Clearly there are some interesting questions to ask about how to relate Christian mission to Old Testament Scripture. If you define mission in terms of presenting (in some way) the claims of Christ, then it is complicated to find examples of that happening in the Old Testament, though obviously there is a long history of reading the Old Testament christologically. If you define mission in terms of joining in with what God is doing—the *missio dei* as it is often put—then clearly you can find models and examples of that all over the Old Testament. The result is that missiologists with an interest in scriptural resources for mission take different routes. For the former, the mighty work of David Bosch, *Transforming Mission*, stands as an example, spending only

4 or 5 pages on the Old Testament out of nearly 600 pages.[2] For the latter see Christopher Wright's *The Mission of God: Unlocking the Bible's Grand Narrative,* which by my estimate spends around two thirds of its 600 pages on the Old Testament.[3]

I have been persuaded by Michael Stroope's remarkable book *Transcending Mission* that basically it all depends on your definition.[4] Stroope shows how Christ-focused definitions reduce the input of the Old Testament, while *missio dei* definitions enlarge it. A third option is to find the missional focus in the way Scripture is read: a *missional hermeneutic*.[5] This almost seems to acknowledge that you will not find mission in the biblical (Old Testament) text unless you choose to go looking for it, though its defendants would say that it highlights things too easily overlooked otherwise.

Stroope actually wants to go further and challenge the language of mission at all: he sees it as a post-biblical term with unfortunate connotations, particularly tied up with colonialism and power, and he advocates (though rather briefly) an alternative language of 'pilgrim witness.'[6] I am sympathetic to his point, though I think it serves better as a reminder of the ever-present danger of projecting our own priorities onto Scripture and calling them 'mission,' rather than requiring us to abandon the language. In fact we might say that abandoning the language ducks some of the issues in addressing past problems in mission practice.[7] In any case, there is little chance of the language of mission fading away any time soon, so I will simply get on with trying to root our mission thinking a bit more securely in some Old Testament texts. Let us turn to the Book of Genesis.

For Reflection

- How do you and your church use 'mission' language in practice?
- What role (if any) has the Old Testament played so far in your thinking about mission?

From Babel to the Rest of the World—Genesis 11 and Mission

2

Something fascinating happens in the tower of Babel story (Gen 11.1–9) that I think can shed a lot of light on our sense of mission in the church today, especially in Western culture in the early twenty-first century. It is right there in the story, in verse 9: 'The LORD scattered them abroad over the face of all the earth' (Gen 11.9).

In this chapter I will read through the Babel story, look at how it fits into Genesis 1–11, and then discuss two ways of reading this particular verse, verse 9. One is more negative, reading the story as being about judgment. The other is more positive, and reads the story as the strange work of God in blessing. The two go together, I suggest, and lead to a profound insight into mission. But first, let us read the story.

Reading the Babel Story[8]

Read Gen 11.1–9

This delightful short story is beautifully told. It begins with the whole earth having 'one language and the same words,' or as the NIV helpfully paraphrases: 'a common speech.' Thoughtful readers will be alerted to something odd going on if they arrive at Genesis 11 fresh from reading Genesis 10, because in Gen 10.5, 20 and 31 we heard about all the nations of the earth (or at least approximately 70 of them) each having their own language.

This is one among many examples of the ways in which stories in Genesis 1–11 serve more as introductory reflections on the scriptural narrative to come, than as historically-orientated accounts of early events in the earth's history. They are designed to give us ways to think about what follows, in the way a good prologue raises all sorts of interesting questions relevant to the book or film or play to come. Indeed, even serious historical accounts of great figures or events in history often start with a chapter that tells a representative story—one that carries some important insight into the person or event about to be described, but plucked out of its original historical context to serve as an opening way in. I have seen this device used in books on topics ranging from Babylon to the Beatles. Genesis did it first.[9]

So for whatever reason, we are now hearing a story about a world of one common language, and setting to one side the world full of 70 nations of different languages that we met in the previous chapter. What do we learn as we do this?

We are reading about a generic 'everyone,' with one generic language, and they travel and act and speak in the story as one. This sounds like a tale with lessons to teach about generic human nature. There is something we need to learn about the role of humans in 'the whole earth' here. We read on.

Eastwards they head (Gen 11.2)—in fact it is unclear whether they are going to or from the East. It does not matter. They arrive at a plain in the land of Shinar. You would have had to be a very alert reader of Genesis 10 to have noticed that in Gen 10.10 we already met 'the land of Shinar,' and we found there the beginnings of Nimrod's kingdom, including a place called Babel. In fact you would also have to have not been reading the NIV, because the NIV of Gen 10.10 says 'Babylon,' not Babel, and here in Gen 11.2 the NIV helps us out with a footnote saying 'that is, Babylonia.' But the story, for reasons that will become clear, is saving up this piece of information for a later reveal, so we too—unlike the NIV—will set it to one side.[10]

The people decide that a great plain in Shinar is just the place for a city and a tower: a tower 'with its top in the heavens' (11.4). It reads like the city is the tower. Or perhaps the tower is the crowning building project of the city. It is certainly odd that this story is universally known as 'the tower of Babel' when in fact the city gets more attention than the tower. Here are all the references:

- Gen 11.4: a city and a tower
- Gen 11.5: the city and the tower
- Gen 11.8: (they left off building) the city
- [Gen 11.9: 'Therefore it was called Babel'—the 'it' seems to be the city?]

In other words, the city is mentioned three times, and the tower twice. I am not imagining that this Grove booklet could change the way we refer to the story, but it really is 'the city of Babel' even more than it is 'the tower of Babel.' We will come back to why this might make a difference.

They get busy with bricks and bitumen, building up a big city / tower. In due course readers of Exodus will find the same phrase about 'making (or perhaps "baking") bricks' in Exod 5.7, in the context of the forced labour of the Israelite slaves trying to fulfil Egyptian building projects using bricks without straw. It is not therefore an overly promising or positive phrase.

The purpose of the city / tower building project is to 'make a name for ourselves' (Gen 11.4), and explicitly they say—that is the generic 'human race' character says—'otherwise we shall be scattered abroad upon the face of the whole earth' (Gen 11.4). Hold that thought. It turns out to be part of the key to the whole story.

Next God enters the story. It is YHWH, the LORD, the named God of Israel, who enters in verse 5, and gets named five times in the five verses that remain. Readers are to make no mistake: this is a story about the God of Israel engaging with the whole human race. Programmatically. What will God do in the face of this almighty human building project?

The first thing God does is make fun of it, almost. God has to 'come down' to see it (Gen 11.5), and says, in an interesting divine plural, 'Come, let us go down…' (Gen 11.7). What to humans feels like a scaling of the heavens is so small that God cannot actually see it clearly until coming down. Another way that God seems to deflate the human project here is with the precise choice of words. Humankind said, in verse 4, 'Come, let us build ourselves a city…' God says, in verse 7, 'Come, let us go down…' Is it almost as if God is hinting that it is not for humans to adopt this impressive royal-sounding way of speaking? This is God's way of speaking! As to what it actually means: if it is not simply a mimicking of human pretension then perhaps it is also an echo of the plural language of Gen 1.26—'Let us make *'adam* [humankind] in our image.' So some say it is a kind of royal plural. Some say it is God consulting with the divine council of angels and celestial beings. Some read a prefiguring of trinitarian language. There is something going for all these theories (though not all at the same time), but it is not particularly relevant to our purposes in reading Gen 11 to decide between them, so we will move on.

The issue with the building project is that humankind is set to follow its own path

The presenting issue with the building project is that generic humankind is set to follow its own path now—'nothing that they propose to do will now be impossible for them' (Gen 11.6). You might want to paraphrase slightly here: 'the sky's the limit!' Literally? They will build and build and never attend to anything but their building. It is truly extraordinary that this critique of human activity is over 2,500 years old, rather than being written in one of today's megalopolises. But then again, Scripture is extraordinary in so many ways.

The divine plan, in verse 7, is to confuse the beloved 'one language' (or 'common speech') with which the story began. So the LORD scatters them over the face of the earth, 'from there' as verse 8 rather pointedly adds (for emphasis?). 'And they left off building the city.' If the narrator had known how this story would be labelled in centuries to come, he would surely have added 'and the tower.' But anyway…Interestingly the story does not explain the link between the confusing of language in verse 7, and the LORD scattering the people abroad in verse 8. Does the language confusion send them out in itself, no longer able to work together? Is it a separate divine action, following on from the language confusion? The narrator does not tell us, and perhaps we do not need to know.

There are two big points to come in the final verse—the two points that make sense of the story and its programmatic purpose in Scripture. They deserve their own sub-headings.

'Babel'

Genesis 11.9 tells us that 'it' (the city / tower) 'was called Babel' because there God 'confused' their language. This is a characteristic piece of wordplay in Hebrew: the verb 'to confuse' is *balal*. John Goldingay draws out the link in his translation in *The Bible for Everyone*: 'It was named Babel, because there Yahweh made a babble of the language of the entire earth.'[11]

Now we circle back to that oblique reference to Shinar in verse 2, and the NIV's determination to spoil the surprise with its footnotes and its translation of Genesis 10. The surprise is this: this story about a mysterious Babel is in fact on some level (also) a story about Babylon. The name Babel and its derivatives occurs nearly 300 times in the Old Testament, and setting to one side the NIV for a moment pretty much all translations use it only twice: here in Gen 11.9 and earlier in Gen 10.10. In all the other occasions—well over 250—it is translated 'Babylon.' So to be fair, all the NIV is doing in Gen 10.10, and with its footnote to Gen 11.2, is starting early with this translation.

The Babel in question in Gen 11.9 is a kind of primeval 'one great city' rather than straightforwardly the later empire of Babylon. The Babylonian empire had two notable periods of expansion and success. The first was under Hammurabi, in the eighteenth-century century BC. Arguably it is never mentioned in Scripture, though perhaps these two Genesis references are in some way alluding to it? The second—and so known as the neo-Babylonian empire—is the one that dominates large parts of the Old Testament: first mentioned in a couple of apparently innocuous warm-up stories in 2 Kings 17 and 20, before it bursts aggressively on to the world stage under the expansionist military policies of its famous king Nebuchadnezzar at the beginning of the sixth century BC, from 2 Kgs 24.1 onwards, relentlessly. Nothing but trouble. This Babylonian empire is the villain of the tragic exile of Israel / Judah in around 587 BC, which leaves its mark on so much Old Testament Scripture, through profound lament, soul-searching, tears and anguish.

Now at this point, the Old Testament scholars get excited and wonder whether perhaps Genesis 11 was *written* in the exile, to address the Babylonian world in which they found themselves, with their great towers (*ziggurats*) to the heavens, their world-building ideology, and their concern to conquer the earth. Well perhaps it was, and it would make sense, all things considered. But in fact we simply do not know when the story was written (as is usually the case in the Old Testament). It is enough to say this: it would have been *read* as part of the introduction to Genesis during and beyond the exile. And whether the writer of the tower (city) of Babel story intended to refer to ancient Babel / Babylon, or was an exilic writer thinking directly about the neo-Babylonian empire, what we can say for sure is that the story runs up against the sixth century Babylonian empire with a spectacular clash of agendas and understandings. Genesis 11.1–9 is seriously saying that the LORD, the God of Israel, will confuse and scatter any who seek to centralize and conquer. It now becomes clear, incidentally, why I think it might have been more helpful to call this story the 'city of Babel'—the city is Babylon, one way or another.

It is an anti-empire text whether the empire was ancient (the first Babylonian empire) or 'modern' (the second Babylonian empire). Of course, that still applies today. Or at least: it still applies if we too live in a world of expansionism, building projects without limit, and colonial mentality…

But like many great Old Testament stories of judgment upon the nations of the world, the judgment also includes Israel too, not in the sense that Israel is somehow marked out as failing (I will come back to the way some views of mission seem to think this), but in the sense that Israel is caught up along with everyone else, caught up into this story about generic (one) humankind. To get at this, we need the second emphasis in Gen 11.9.

Scattering

The result of the city / tower of Babel story is clear: 'the LORD scattered them abroad over the face of all the earth' (Gen 11.9). However we relate this story to the table of nations in Genesis 10, by the end of Gen 11.1–9 we do indeed have people of many languages spread out in many places, just as Genesis 10 described it.

But the feature of the story that gives pause for thought here is that this scattering ends up fulfilling part of the very purpose of the creation of humankind in Genesis 1. In Gen 1.28, right after the creation of *'adam* (humankind) in Gen 1.27, as 'male and female,' we read:

> God blessed them, and God said to them,
> 'Be fruitful
> and multiply,
> and fill the earth

and subdue it;
and have dominion.'[12] (over fish / birds / land animals)

This five-fold mandate, which is also a blessing, marks out key aspects of the calling to be human on God's earth. The fourth one has caused considerable concern among ecologically-minded interpreters of Genesis, since 'subdue' is a somewhat domineering word most of the time in the OT. Maybe the unruly scope of the ancient natural world simply did require aggressive forms of 'caring'? But this is not our present focus and in fact does not particularly make a difference to the point I am making in this section about scattering. (Personally I would love it if it turned out that Genesis 1 was all for ecological sensitivity regarding taking care of the creation, but while most of it is, I am not persuaded that all of it is.)[13]

The first three of the five verbs are more straightforward: to be fruitful and to multiply are either two things that include reproducing, or one thing, which is fruitfully to reproduce. Either way, they lead to 'filling the earth.' The fourth and fifth verbs, positive or negative in scope as they may be with regard to creature care and creation care, both involve getting out and about and attending to the life of the animals in the creation, and the land that will be found there.

It is in this context that repopulating the world after the flood, and 'spreading abroad' (NRSV) after the Babel story, take on a more positive tone. Genesis 9.19 tells us that from the three sons of Noah 'the whole earth was peopled' (NRSV). The verb here translated 'peopled' is a little ambiguous, and the NIV and ESV handle it in a different way: 'from them came the people who were scattered over the whole earth' (NIV), or likewise 'from these the people of the whole earth were dispersed' (ESV).[14]

Gen 10.18 uses the exact same verb as Gen 11's 'scattering': 'the families of the Canaanites spread abroad' (NRSV) or—again—'scattered' (NIV) / 'dispersed' (ESV). This operates as a soft build-up to Genesis 11 in much the same way that the oddity about multiple / one language(s) does. We thus arrive at the Babel story to be struck afresh by the unexpected outcome of all this tower and city building being put to ruin:

> Gen 11.4: 'otherwise we shall be scattered,' say humankind
> Gen 11.8: 'so the LORD scattered them'
> Gen 11.9: 'the LORD scattered them'

Three times in the short story we find this emphasis on scattering, in direct contrast to the human desire to consolidate and build up their tower / city / reputation…

And so it comes to pass that humankind ends the tower/city of Babel story fulfilling (rather inadvertently) the creation mandate in Gen 1.28 to get out there and take on the project of attending to God's world, rather than building their own.

Scattered Blessing

As a matter of observation, the two predominant ways of reading the Babel story have traditionally tended towards Jewish interpreters seeing the positive implications of being sent out (scattered) for the sake of attending to God's creation, while Christian interpreters have tended to see the negative implications of the story as being primarily about divine judgment.[15] Were I to preach on this story, and I have, I would actually try to combine both emphases, since I think they are both there in the text. The scattering itself may not be positive, but its impact seems to be. The result is an emphasis on finding God's blessing in and through judgment, which is demanding but—if Genesis 11 is to be believed—life-giving not just for ourselves but for all the world.

Finding God's blessing in and through judgment is life-giving

It may be that our church or mission project (whether a building project or whatever kind of ministry project it is) seems to run aground on what feels like divine confounding of all our efforts. I have certainly known such projects myself, some of which I put a considerable amount of energy into. It becomes tempting to think that better planning and more capable execution was what was needed. But sometimes (or indeed, often?) there may be a deeper reality at work: God appears simply not interested in my project succeeding, and in the confounding of it God scatters me to play a much more life-giving role than I myself had considered in all my planning and effort.

Let me broaden the point to Christian mission work more generally. I have lived and moved in the world of Christian mission, at home and abroad, in various ways, over many years. I have friends who have been much more invested in it than me, and who do much more remarkable things than I have ever done. But my experience, and that of many of my mission-minded friends and colleagues, is that there is often not a straightforward match between what we planned and what ended up happening. My reading of Genesis 11 suggests that this is not a disaster to be lamented, except possibly in the sense that we maybe planned some poorly conceived projects, I suppose. Instead it is in the resulting scattering that we may become the blessing to God's world that we were hoping to be anyway.

I arrive at the conclusion of this study of the city / tower of Babel story. To put the point concisely: in the midst of what looks like judgment comes divine blessing. We think we know what success will look like, but how often are we completely wrong, in theological terms? What we overlook is the divine purpose to be found in scattering us.

So I find myself wanting to articulate a model of mission that revolves around *scattered blessing*. Humankind (the generic 'they' of the Babel story) is not quick to think of the ways to serve God's mission in the world around us. Sometimes we need to be pushed out, away from our empire-building, to find renewed life and purpose in places far from our comfort zones or familiar environments. When that happens, the story of what God is doing in and through us is just beginning. The city / tower of Babel story is not fundamentally a disaster that results in an ending, though it does include disaster and ending. Rather it is a beginning: a gateway through which the whole story of Scripture takes off—in new and remarkably world-transforming directions.

For Reflection

- Can you think of examples in your own missional and ministerial work where you have experienced the 'positive' sense of being scattered (as a blessing) and the 'negative' sense (as a judgment)?
- What are some of the ways we can see blessing in and through judgment in our own lives and ministry?

From Abraham to the Rest of the World—Genesis 12 and Mission

3

The claim about the tower of Babel story and its model of scattered blessing, in the previous chapter, is not a common one in Christian understandings of mission. This is partly because, as I noted, Christians have tended towards reading the Babel story primarily as being about judgment, in contrast to Jewish readings that discern the blessings amidst being scattered. There is something to ponder there in the way that the Jewish tradition, with its persistent experience of exile or marginalization, may be more alert to such an emphasis on the blessings of being scattered. We will return to this towards the end when we think through what Christian readings might learn here about their own self-understanding in terms of power and agency.

But there is another reason why Gen 11.1–9 has been obscured in mission thinking, and that is the presence of another text, one short chapter later, that has been co-opted into playing a major role in an understanding of Old Testament mission. This other text is Gen 12.1–3, or to some extent Gen 12.1–9. Among Christian missiologists, this text carries a remarkable weight, almost as if it is a mandate for the whole of Scripture's story being read as a story about mission.[16]

Now I am not going to say that Gen 12.1–3 is not capable of being read this way. Perhaps it too offers a model of mission that can inform Christian practice. In fact the model it offers looks at first sight a lot like the model of scattered blessing that I have been sketching out in the previous chapter. But the differences are instructive, and in the end significant. So here I will read this text carefully, much as we read Gen 11.1–9 above, and then draw some different conclusions.

Reading the Story

Read Gen 12.1–9

Not much has happened since we stopped at Gen 11.9. Or alternatively, a whole world of change has happened—sometimes it is hard to tell in Genesis. If Genesis 1–11 is indeed the prologue to Scripture, as I suggested, then it functions a bit like a pre-credits sequence, most famously turned into an art form in James Bond movies where it feels like a whole film's worth of budget has gone into a spectacular opening scene, and it takes a while to work out how it relates to what follows. Of course, what follows such a sequence is the credits. Lo and behold, that is roughly what takes up the rest of Genesis 11: verses 10–32 give us a genealogy through the descendants of Noah's son Shem, all the way down to Abram. Ten generations, more or less with two verses per generation, in a formulaic way, as we zoom down from ancient prehistory to ancient history, with the camera fading back up on Abram to start to tell us a good long proper story.

When the author of Chronicles got to this bit, they reduced it all to ten words: just the list of the ten names and no other detail mattered (1 Chron 1.24–27), except the bit about Abram being the same person as Abraham, which Genesis does not get to until Gen 17.5. For simplicity's sake, and because the issue about his name plays no real part in what I want to talk about, I will call him Abraham here except where directly quoting Genesis 12.[17]

Fade up, then, on Genesis 12, with all we know being that humankind is now scattered across the earth, and Abraham—along with a few close family members (Gen 11.31)—has left Ur of the Chaldeans, which is south east of Babylon, even further into what is now modern Iraq than Babylon was, and settled in Haran, which is north, even though the family was apparently heading to the land of Canaan. Genesis 11.31 gives no sense of why they stopped short. Perhaps it was better up north than they had thought, let the (British) reader understand.

I find descriptions of journeys like this hard to follow without a map, so here is a map (see Figure 1)[18]

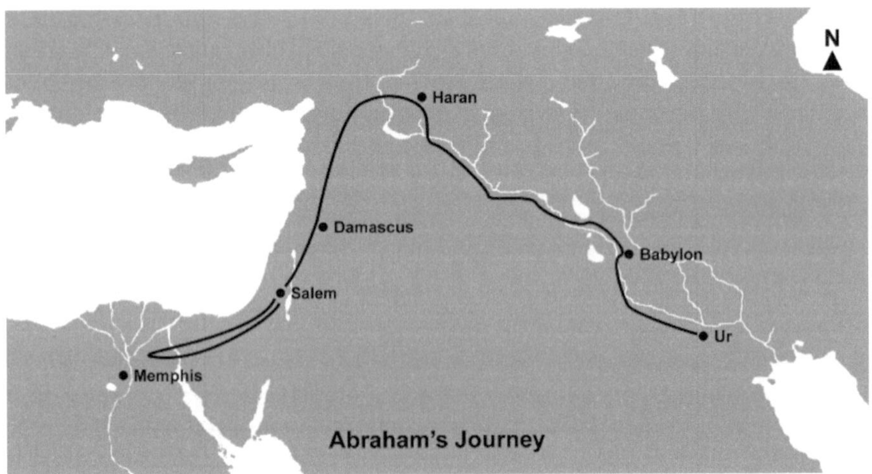

Figure 1 Abraham's Journey in Genesis 12

I am not quite sure why this map mentions Damascus (where Abraham's servant Eliezer is from [Gen 15.2]), or Salem (where King Melchizedek is in charge [Gen 14.18]), or Memphis, which only gets mentioned in the Bible in the prophets, but to be fair may have been a (the?) major city at that time in Egypt, which is where Abraham is headed by Gen 12.10. But it does show, with elegant simplicity, the scale that Abraham's journey involved.

One of the interesting things here from a mission point of view, of course, is that we are on the move. Wherever and whenever the stories of Genesis 1–11 took place, this is now a story that we can trace on a map, and relate to the world as we know it (more or less). I suspect this is part of the reason why Genesis 12 looms large in mission-minded appeals to the Old Testament. Ever since the rise of modern means of transport played their part in facilitating the rise of the modern missions movement, travel—or more simply *going*—has been seen as a key element of mission. Granted 'Go!' is one of the keywords used in Jesus' so-called Great Commission in Matthew 28 (v 19), even if it is not the main verb of the relevant passage. As is often noted, Matt 28.19 can be read as 'Going [or 'as you go'], make disciples...baptize...and teach...'—so that the three core activities are the making disciples, baptizing and teaching. Interestingly, this verse / passage only became a central biblical text for mission in modern times, as David Bosch showed in his fascinating treatment of appeals to Scripture in the history of the church's mission.[19] Most reformers thought it had been fulfilled by the early church, for instance.[20]

However, if you are primed to look for the importance of 'Go!' or 'going,' then Genesis 12 hits you squarely between the eyes:

> 'Now the LORD said to Abram,
> "Go from your country
> and your kindred
> and your father's house
> to the land that I will show you."' (Gen 12.1)

Some amazing texts of divine promise follow, which we will look at in a minute, but no sooner are they reported, than we read in verse 4: 'So Abram went, as the LORD had told him...'

The LORD says 'Go!' and Abraham went. Could it be any clearer? In fact it *is* clearer. The form of 'Go!' here is a rare idiomatic usage: *lek-lᵉka,* which is something like 'Go [to] yourself...' Goldingay's *Bible for Everyone* offers, 'Get yourself from your country...' I wonder if we should say 'Get yourself gone!' Or 'Get up and go,' which is not exactly how Gen 12.1 says it, but is the point. This idiomatic usage is so rare that it only occurs one other time in Scripture, at the beginning of Genesis 22 (verse 2), where God says to Abraham (and

Isaac) 'Get yourself gone to the land of Moriah,' at the start of the gruelling and unforgettable passage about God's testing of Abraham, with regard to whether he would be willing to sacrifice his son. (Spoiler: he is, but does not have to.) Is the phrase designed to draw attention to Abraham's faithful obedience in some way?

In short, if we are looking for a story where the emphasis—or part of the emphasis—is on obedience to the call to go, then Gen 12.1–4 (and following) is likely to be a favourite text. In a moment we will ask whether we *should* be looking for such a text. But first we turn to the promises of Gen 12.2–3, which are interposed between the call and the obedient response, and thus are therefore clearly programmatic in some way for what the call of Abraham is all about. In some way or other, it is all about blessing.

Blessing

The densely packed sentence in Gen 12.2–3 unfolds into seven component parts as the LORD continues to speak to Abraham:

1 [2] I will make of you a great nation,
2 and I will *bless* you,
3 and make your name great,
4 so that you will be a *blessing*.
5 [3] I will *bless* those who *bless* you,
6 and the one who curses you I will curse;
7 and in you all the families of the earth shall be *blessed*.

The five-fold emphasis on blessing cannot be missed. It has even been suggested that this five-fold blessing emphasis is a significant response to five mentions of 'curse' in Genesis 1–11.[21] The vocabulary of 'cursing' in Genesis 12 actually varies—the ESV is one of the few translations to capture this in line 6 when it says 'him who dishonours you I will curse.'[22]

But there are two complications before we pronounce that we have uncovered the purpose of this passage—a purpose that is easily and frequently summarized as 'Go and be a blessing to all the nations!' Much as with my comment on Gen 1.28 above, I would be delighted if that is what Genesis 12 said, because who would not want to see as many nations as possible blessed? But I am not sure it is what it says.

The first complication is the opaque nature of what blessing is, even just restricting ourselves to English usage. In priestly contexts, of which Num 6.24–26 would be an obvious example (the so-called Aaronic blessing), to bless is something specific: to bring about the life-giving presence of God in the life of the one blessed. That the presence of God could be influenced, let alone determined, by a priest's say-so is not something that many modern Christians find easy to understand, but it does seem to have been the intent of Num 6.24–26. But not all blessing takes place in priestly contexts, even in the Old Testament, and Genesis 12 is a prime example of this more widely-shared sense of blessing. Perhaps it will suffice to say that blessing is the invocation of God's life-giving presence, without trying to be too specific as to how it is (or is not) determined by the words of blessing used. It is clearly a good thing. To bless is to celebrate the life-giving power of God's presence with a person or in a situation, and to speed it on its (or their) life-giving way.[23]

How Abraham embodies such blessing in the Book of Genesis is—to say the least—not always obvious, as Pharaoh might be reflecting even before Genesis 12 is done.

But a further complication is that the Hebrew idioms used here do not seem to work the way we might expect them to, based on our loose English understanding. Line 4 says that the result of God's blessing is that Abraham will 'be a blessing.' The construction involves an imperative: 'Be a blessing!' We might have an English-language sense of saying, 'It was a blessing to have Abe on the team,' and in that sense Abe was 'a blessing.' But there is no example in Hebrew of blessing language being used this way. The Hebrew sense of the phrase is that Abraham's name will be used as a blessing by others.

The purpose of Abraham being a blessing is told by verse 3: culminating (in line 7) with 'in you all the families of the earth shall be blessed.' Much has been written on how to handle the verb 'bless' (*bārak*) here. I shall attempt a brisk summary: the form of *bārak* that occurs here in Gen 12.3c also occurs in Gen 18.18 and Gen 28.14, and it is ambiguous grammatically. It could be:

- a reflexive sense ('shall bless themselves')
- a passive sense ('shall be blessed') = KJV, NRSV, ESV, NIV, in various ways
- or possibly a middle sense: 'shall find blessing'

A different, and definitely reflexive, form of *bārak* occurs at Gen 22.18 and Gen 26.4, in verses that look like they have the same function as Gen 12.3c, describing a relationship between all the families/nations of the earth, and the blessing to Abraham. Indeed in the case of 26.4 it is deliberately referring back to the earlier occasion. Thus if the meaning is consistent throughout all of Gen 12.3c, Gen 22.18 and Gen 26.4, we would expect that the verb in Gen 12.3c should be translated as per the reflexive sense of *bārak*, and hence: 'all the families of the earth shall bless themselves.'

But what does this mean? In essence, it means that people will pray to be blessed like God has blessed Abraham. A good example of blessing being understood this way is Gen 48.20, where the patriarch Jacob blesses Joseph's sons by saying to each of them, 'By [*or:* in] you Israel will invoke blessings, saying "God make you like Ephraim and like Manasseh."' To be a blessing to others, in these terms, is to be an example of a blessed person. This in turn may then point people to the God who has blessed oneself.

I am indebted here and throughout this discussion of Gen 12.3 to the careful interpretative work of Walter Moberly, whose key emphasis is that in context Gen 12.1–3 offers overwhelming assurance to Abraham and his family as they set out alone and under-resourced into an unknown world. As the nations watch him go, will they then say to themselves, 'We want to be like Abraham'? Which may then lead to, 'We want to know the God who is blessing that man…'—*ie* they may 'bless themselves.' Some writers give the impression that this is a more or less trivial way of receiving the import of Gen 12.3, missing the supposed programmatic missional impact of this passage, but I let Moberly's own words summarize the matter in response:

> If one reads the text not from the perspective of Christian faith seeking Old Testament warrant for Christian universalism or mission, but from the imagined perspective of Abraham, and implicitly of the nation that descends from him, then it looks different. Those who respond to the costly call of God to leave behind what they have, and whose subsequent way of living will set them apart from their neighbours and perhaps provoke antagonism, do not regard a divine reassurance that God will bless them and give them positive recognition as in any way trivial. Rather, it engenders a hope that will sustain them through difficult times.[24]

Cross-cultural mission workers, interestingly enough, may be uniquely well-placed to grasp that point, and to be greatly encouraged by it.

For Reflection

- What do you think 'blessing' is (a) in your own context? (b) in the Bible?
- How does the example of Abraham in Genesis 12 help us understand mission in the case of (a) those who have travelled across the world to serve God? (b) those who have remained to serve God geographically where they already were?

Two Points of Comparison—Power and Jewish-Christian Relations 4

So far I have argued that Genesis 11 offers a model of scattered blessing. Then Genesis 12 offers a model that—to summarize it awkwardly—is about going in such a way that others are provoked to seek blessing. Both passages envisage people heading out to a life spread abroad—among the nations, as the Old Testament tends to put it. Both passages, significantly, draw in notions of blessing.

Perhaps, then, we have here two models of mission? I am not going to say that one is right and the other is wrong. Both passages offer profound and life-giving insight into living for God across the face of creation, as you might expect given the nature and purposes of holy Scripture. But I do want to draw out some ways in which I think that the Genesis 11 model—scattered blessing—might be a useful corrective to over-concentration on the Genesis 12 one—on going in the service of blessing.

Some issues that I think most helpfully clarify what is at stake are power (or agency), the related question of intentional going, and the tricky issue of Jewish-Christian relationships when Old Testament texts (which are also of course Jewish Scripture texts) are being related to Christian mission concerns.

Power and Agency in Christian Mission

The role of power in mission has a long and vexed history, and I only want to add one small note to it. Notice that in the tower of Babel story the protagonists (the human race) are not in charge of their destiny. They are scattered—a passive verb. Scattering is what happens to them, and they find themselves spread across the face of the whole earth (Gen 11.4), far from the envisaged comforts of their tower / city complex. There is something achingly vulnerable about the result: in so far as Genesis 11 sees a successful fulfilling of the creation mandate to fill the earth (and so to care for it), it is a scenario in which all the initiative lies with God. If this is mission, then the agency involved—the question of who takes all the initiative—lies not with those sent out, but squarely with the God who sends them. In one sense I do think this is a deliberate feature of the story: humans set themselves up to know what they should do, but actually it is what God wants to do that will end up determinative.

The missional call in the light of this might be: you will not be advised to 'Go!' but you will end up going anyway, to wherever God takes you. Do not presume to know why you are going, but once you get to wherever it is, look for the reasons that God has put you there.[25] And there *will* be God-given ways in to the opportunities you find, as Gen 1.28 made clear. This scattered blessing model of going is thus explicit about recognizing God as being the one who distributes us around the world, in whatever manner of going we end up undertaking.

Obviously Gen 12.1–3 can also be read as being all about God's initiative in sending Abraham, with the added element of going 'to the land that I will show you' (Gen 12.1). But the emphasis is different. To over-simplify for the sake of clarity: Genesis 11 involves a passive 'being scattered,' while Genesis 12 involves an active 'going.' Both are the work of God, but the second can be owned and planned for, while the first happens to you. This is the difference that makes a difference.

Going: The Nature of Being Sent

Another difference is that the kind of going that Genesis 11's scattering involves is not fundamentally about travel, nor indeed international travel. Intentional international travel may be a wonderful thing, though interestingly the ecological cost of such travel is currently forcing a bit of a rethink. But travel as such, I want to say, is largely incidental to the nature and tasks of Christian mission. It fitted neatly with the modern world's excitement about discovering hitherto unreached territories. But it is almost a modern-era red herring, one that led us to interpret the Great Commission's lead-word 'Go!' in too central a way. Note for example that the early church's standard reading of Gen 12.1–3 was in terms of an allegory about 'all those who undertake the spiritual journey.'[26] The modern overemphasis on physical going rendered mission a little too easily as a project that took people from (a) Christian cultures to (b) unchristian cultures. In turn that then too easily drifted into all the implications of power (and colonialism) that can arise when mission is seen as the geographical transfer of the gospel.

In my view one of the most perceptive accounts of the possibilities that lie beyond this picture was David Smith's turn-of-the-century account of *Mission after Christendom*, which relocated the mission frontiers not as geographical borders but as the interfaces of Christian faith with secularization, pluralization and globalization.[27] Christians are still sent (or, perhaps better 'called') to engage with these issues, but the prominence of physical travel has disappeared.[28]

The language of calling, incidentally, is also a lot more promising biblically. As far as I can discover, Israel is never 'sent' (*shālach*) to anywhere or anyone in the Old Testament: prophets are sent, usually within Israel; Israel is 'sent away' (*ie* into exile—Jer 3.8; 24.5; 29.4), or, rarely, 'given,' as we shall see in a moment.

I sometimes use the following diagram (Figure 2) to help students and congregations begin to think about the multiple ways in which the Old Testament story actually seems to prefer casting the people of God just as much as 'those to whom history happens' as 'those who make history.' (These are clumsy labels, I know, but I hope the point is clear.)

Prologue: *Genesis 1–11*

First Version

Genesis 12.1–3 → Moses (law) → David (& Kings) → Prophets →...

Second Version

Genesis 11.1–9

↓

Israel against the empires: Egypt (15th–13th century)

Assyria (8th century)

Babylon (late 7th/6th century)

Persia (6th–4th century)

↓

...

Figure 2 Two Ways of Looking at the Big Story of the Old Testament

We have probably got past the stage of triumphalism in Christian mission now, though sadly I think this has often happened because of struggling with the difficulties of seeing any sense of triumph work out in practice. Had the Old Testament offered more of a guide to some aspects of mission thinking, perhaps it would have been clear that triumph was never supposed to be a realistic goal anyway. How often was Israel in a position of self-determination? Only rarely. But scattered among the nations, whether from Babel or, painfully, in the exile, or even beyond, its faithful witness to the God of the whole earth persisted.[29] For which we Christians are to give thanks.

Christian Mission as the Fulfilment of Israel's Calling?

A second reflection concerns the awkward ways in which Christian appeals to Gen 12.1–3 in mission sometimes handle the nature of Jewish and Christian identity. To put it bluntly: some Christian missiologists play up the sinfulness to be found in Genesis 1–11, in order to raise the profile of hope and blessing in Gen 12.1–3. There is considerable precedent for this way of reading Genesis in twentieth-century Old Testament scholarship, notably from von Rad, and those who follow him.[30] When it is tied to a sense of *Christian* mission as the fulfilment of Gen 12.1–3, then the unfortunate impression can be given that the Jewish faith and tradition is darkness and poorly understood hope—*for* the nations, yes, but not particularly understood or embraced—until Christians came along and got it right.[31]

The fundamental thing to say here is this: we need to be a whole lot more careful in how we, as Christians, say that God chose Israel for the sake of the nations. Perhaps the nearest the Old Testament comes to saying this is Isa 49.6, though this is a subtle passage: the servant is Israel in Isa 49.3, but has a task to restore Israel in Isa 49.6a. Whoever the servant is, in Isa 49.6b it is 'given as'/'made to be' (the verb is *nātan*, not *shālach*, 'to send') a light to the nations/Gentiles (*goyîm*). This is indeed wonderful, but should not be overread as giving the biblical account of why God chose Israel.

God chose Israel because God loves Israel

In the sense that it is true that God chose Israel for the sake of the nations, it is the *second* thing we are to say. The *first* thing we are to say is this: God chose Israel because God loves Israel. I cannot explain *why* this is so. I do not think Israel can either. Probably the core text expressing (grateful) bafflement on this issue is Deut 7.7–8: 'It was not because you were more numerous than any other people that the Lord set his heart on you and chose you—for you were the fewest of all peoples. It was because the Lord loved you…' Or in other words: God loved you because he loved you. Jewish scholars celebrate Israel's election as God's beloved people, and are happy to hear (by and large) that God's love overflows even to Gentiles, but that is not, in their view, the point or purpose of God's love for Israel.[32]

Christians want to go on and say more than this, not least in light of texts such as Gal 3.8, where good news for the Gentiles is foreseen in the promise to Abraham. But this wider (and wonderful) overflowing is not the same as saying that the *purpose* of Abraham's call was to bless the nations.

The mission model of scattered blessing that I am advocating looks a lot like how Israel in the Old Testament went about its life and calling in the sight of the nations. Then, as now, there were/are wonderful examples, mixed in with poor examples, of faithfulness to God. Neither Jewish nor Christian believers have a monopoly on getting it right, nor on getting it wrong. There was life-giving goodness to be found in Genesis 1–11, along with sin. Just like in the rest of the Old Testament, and likewise in the New Testament. Genesis 12.1–3, on this reading, is one more example of God at work, along with human faithful response. It is not the key to mission in Scripture, or a missiological focus for all our Bible reading, or any of the other all-encompassing things that are sometimes said for it. It is, like the blessing to be found in and through the Babel story, a source of blessing. And that is enough.

For Reflection

- How often in your own ministry can you see direct links between what you planned and fruitful results? And how often are such links very hard to find?
- Does the argument of this chapter resonate with your understandings of the gospels and Acts or not? What NT examples might there be where people (a) successfully executed their mission plans? or (b) failed to do so but ended up bringing blessing to people anyway?

(If you are discussing these questions in a group, it may be particularly helpful with these questions to think about the range of different answers you have between you.)

5 Scattered Blessings—A Personal and Practical Reflection

So in practice…

You will ask: where are the five marks of mission?[33] One will say 'Look—here they are!,' and another 'Look, there they are!' but they will already be among you.

I have done door-to-door evangelism, ranging from 'Hello, we are from the local church and would like to invite you to our carol service' right through to rather more heavy-handed versions. And thus I have sat in carpeted living rooms or huddled on frozen front steps and tried to cajole people into the kingdom, from a standing start. I did street preaching, I organized mission talks, I ran outreach projects…Trying to bring God into the hard places.

But then I have stopped and asked whether *God might not be there already*? And it is my life which is being spun out—scattered—into just some of the places where God wanted me to be a blessing, so that people might bless themselves. It has transformed my sense of mission. So the heart starts to beat faster, and the spirit quickens, in the low-key, the local, the familiar, the forlorn…

I am sitting with Arnold through the long silences after his wife left him. I am telling the congregation that God is already in their workplaces, and they should ask most for open eyes to see what he is up to. I am standing with Bill in his kitchen, inviting him round to eat because he has no food, and we are standing because the only furniture is his fridge, which is empty, and his son is out again because there is, quite literally, nothing to do at home. I am on my church's free Christmas-present wrapping table at the local shopping centre. Why is this 14-year-old buying his girlfriend lingerie? We talk about that. I think he would rather be anywhere else. Maybe this conversation will bear fruit in his life, though he gives me no encouragement to think so. I sit with Clive who wants to get baptized, and I ask him why. He has no idea. We peel away the family pressures, and talk about Jesus and his life and death and resurrection. By the end: he still wants to get baptized…but I think he now has a vision for what it might mean. The youth group ask me to speak at their 'revival evening.' It is cold and windy, and not well attended. We struggle through songs that do not seem to fill the space, but there is a peace. I talk about Elijah and the still voice of silence: God not in the wind. As I say that, a sudden wind blows through the church and flings the front door open and shakes the space. It lasts a second. Did that really happen? I sit on the floor with the Sparklers, my Sunday school 5–7-year-old group. We pray for pets and PlayStations and finally we pray for Daniella, who says quietly that her prayer is that her Daddy will come back. We pray; and he does not come back; but every week we are cross-legged on the floor, and we smile at her, and we are there for her, and she likes being there. A close friend's son is treated shamefully by a tired and angry teacher at a school event. I arrange to see the head—I dread the meeting—but I try to hold the line at 'Whatever punishment is deserved, you must never shame the children.' It ruins my relationship with the school, and I am not sure anyone except the mum ever thanks me. But he was never shamed again. And then of course there are the sick who stay sick; the blind who still will not see; and the thousand-and-one reasons every day to give up…

But there are bigger reasons to keep going, always: that God is good, Christ is raised from the dead, and the very fact of the church is itself evidence that the new creation is beginning. And in the Old Testament, often and everywhere, are stories, laments, hallelujahs and character portraits of the life of faithful mission to which God calls us: a life of scattered blessing. Proclaiming, nurturing, responding to need, seeking society's transformation, safeguarding creation: the marks have long been among us. We work to share the gift of eyes to see them.

For Reflection

- What stories can you tell about being a 'scattered blessing' to others?
- Are there times and places in the days and weeks to come when you can share your stories to encourage others?

Notes

1 I Paul, *The New Testament's Vision of Mission* (Grove Mission and Evangelism booklet MEv 138).

2 D J Bosch, *Transforming Mission: Paradigm Shifts in Theology of Mission* (Maryknoll, NY: Orbis Books, 1991) pp 16–20.

3 C J H Wright, *The Mission of God: Unlocking the Bible's Grand Narrative* (Nottingham: InterVarsity Press, 2006).

4 M W Stroope, *Transcending Mission: The Eclipse of a Modern Tradition* (London: Apollos, 2017). This one is only 500 pages. What is it with missiologists and big books?

5 *ibid*, pp 41–53.

6 *ibid*, pp 355–385.

7 I was helped to see this by Mark Oxbrow's review of M W Stroope, *Transcending Mission, op cit*, in *Transformation* 37 (2020) pp 83–85.

8 For a more technical study of the story see my 'The Book of Genesis,' in R S Briggs and J N Lohr (eds), *A Theological Introduction to the Pentateuch: Interpreting the Torah as Christian Scripture* (Grand Rapids, MI: Baker Academic, 2012) pp 19–50, especially pp 37–49.

9 See further my 'Humans in the Image of God and Other Things Genesis Does Not Make Clear,' *Journal of Theological Interpretation* 4 (2010) pp 111–126, where I argue that this is what the obscure references to 'image of God' in Genesis 1–9 are doing, for example.

10 Shinar is mentioned 8 times in the OT. Four of them are early in Genesis (Gen 10.10; 11.2; 14.1, 9). Of the others perhaps the most interesting is Dan 1.2, where Nebuchadnezzar takes the spoils from the sacking of the temple 'to the land of Shinar.' It is clearly Babylon, which is named as such around 17 times in the Book of Daniel.

11 I have also seen it translated 'baffle': 'YHWH baffled the language of all the earth-folk'—E Fox, *The Five Books of Moses* (Dallas, TX: Word, 1995) p 49.

12 This is the NRSV translation. The dominion is described as being over sea creatures, flying things and all living things that creep about. I always think this bit of Gen 1 loses something in translation.

13 The fourth verb is *kābash*—to subdue, dominate, bring into bondage. It occurs 14 times in the OT, and is generally a verb with less than life-giving overtones, whether with regard to the subduing of the promised land (Num 32.22, 29; Josh 18.1; and compare 2 Sam 8.11; 1 Chr 22.18); or the enslavement of people (2 Chr 28.10; Neh 5.5 (twice)) or even Haman assaulting Esther (Est 7.8). Compare also 4 uses in the prophets (Jer 34.11, 16; Mic 7.19; Zech 9.15). It is therefore difficult to see it as having a positive sense in Genesis 1, though I guess not impossible.

14 For discussion of the translation options see my 'Book of Genesis' in R S Briggs and J N Lohr (eds), *A Theological Introduction to the Pentateuch, op cit,* p 47 n 70.

15 I find the two traditions mentioned discernible in, respectively, P M Sherman, *Babel's Tower Translated: Genesis 11 and Ancient Jewish Interpretation*, Biblical Interpretation Series 117 (Leiden: Brill, 2013) and A LaCocque, *The Captivity of Innocence: Babel and the Yahwist* (Eugene, OR: Cascade Books, 2010).

16 This is particularly true of C J H Wright, *The Mission of God, op cit*, pp 194-221, and also W C Kaiser Jr, *Mission in the Old Testament: Israel as a Light to the Nations* (Grand Rapids, MI: Baker Books, 2000) pp 17-21 (revised edition 2012, pp 9-12), and M W Goheen, *A Light to the Nations: The Missional Church and the Biblical Story* (Grand Rapids, MI: Baker Academic, 2011) pp 26-32.

17 Apart from Neh 9.7, which is also about the name change, the name 'Abram' is never used again in Scripture after Gen 17.5. In other words, Scripture also calls him 'Abraham,' even in retrospect, once that name is given.

18 This map is from https://www.aionianbible.org/Maps, listed as freely usable and in the public domain. I offer no comment on the Aionian Bible project other than appreciation for its maps.

19 D Bosch, *Transforming Mission, op cit*, pp 339-341. On p 340 he says it is William Carey who raises Matt 28.19-20 to prominence.

20 See R E Davies, 'The Great Commission from Calvin to Carey,' *Evangel* 14.2 (1996) pp 44-49.

21 See H W Wolff, 'The Kerygma of the Yahwist,' in W Brueggemann and H W Wolff, *The Vitality of Old Testament Traditions* (Atlanta, GA: John Knox Press, 1975) pp 41-66, here p 54. The five references to 'curse' (*'arar*) are Gen 3.14; 3.17; 4.11; 5.29 (referring back to 3.17) and 9.25.

22 'Dishonour' here is a form of the verb *qālal*.

23 The excellent introductory study of K Grüneberg, *Blessing: Biblical Meaning and Pastoral Practice.* (Grove Biblical booklet B 27) suggests blessing could be 'God's favour resulting in human prosperity' (p 26) but helpfully shows how hard it is to define.

24 R W L Moberly, *The Theology of the Book of Genesis*, Old Testament Theology (Cambridge University Press, 2009) p 150.

25 Readers familiar with it will spot the resonances with V Donovan, *Christianity Rediscovered* (London: SCM Press, 1978).

26 See the many witnesses gathered in M Sheridan (ed), *Genesis 12-50*. Ancient Christian Commentary on Scripture OT2 (Downers Grove, IL: InterVarsity Press, 2002) pp 1-4. The quotation is from Antony the Great, p 1.

27 D Smith, *Mission After Christendom* (London: Darton, Longman and Todd, 2003).

28 Smith is positive about modern (geographically mapped) mission, (it was 'amazingly successful in its time') but thinks that it 'has almost reached the end of its life.' *ibid*, pp 116-117.

29 The latter part of Daniel expands the focus to the Ptolemaic and Seleucid empires of the thrid and second centuries BC.

30 The books listed in note 16 all do this to some extent.

31 Oddly I was in the middle of writing this Grove booklet when our informal Durham Old Testament studies reading group circulated for discussion a piece by C Cornell, 'Israel's Priority in Old Testament Missiology,' *Missiology: An International Review* 51 (2023) pp 347–360, which makes this point well, in dialogue with Gen 12.1–3 and its interpreters.

32 For a classic statement see J D Levenson, 'The Universal Horizon of Biblical Particularism,' in M G Brett (ed), *Ethnicity and the Bible*, Biblical Interpretation Series 19 (Leiden: Brill,1996) pp 143–169. See also J S Kaminsky, *Yet I Loved Jacob: Reclaiming the Biblical Concept of Election* (Nashville, TN: Abingdon, 2007).

33 See, for example, https://www.anglicancommunion.org/mission/marks-of-mission.aspx